ODDS and EVENS

ODDS and EVENS

BY THOMAS C. O'BRIEN
Illustrated by Allan Eitzen

THOMAS Y. CROWELL COMPANY
NEW YORK

YOUNG MATH BOOKS

Edited by Dr. Max Beberman,
Director of the Committee on School Mathematics Projects,
University of Illinois

Manufactured in the United States of America

L.C. Card 79-106575
ISBN 0-690-59069-5
0-690-59070-9(LB)

2   3   4   5   6   7   8   9   10

ODDS and EVENS

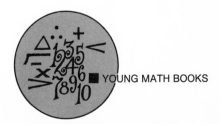

YOUNG MATH BOOKS

There are many types of animals.
There are lions.
And tigers.
And zebras.
And giraffes.

There are many types of people.
There are old people.
There are young people.
There are Indians.

There are Norwegians.
There are doctors.
And there are schoolchildren.

Just as there are many types of people and many types of animals, there are many types of numbers.

Some numbers are even numbers. And some numbers are odd numbers.

Six shoes are an
even number of shoes.

Five shoes are an
odd number of shoes.

Even numbers are important. When you play a game, you usually have an even number of players in the game.

On a basketball team there are 5 players. And 5 is an odd number.

But when two basketball teams play, there is an even number of players in the game. There are 10 players.

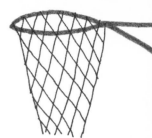

Why is 10 an even number?

Odd numbers are important, too.

Suppose there were 4 people in your family. And suppose the family voted to decide whether they should go north or south on their vacation.

With an even number of voters, it is possible that no clear-cut decision could be made. Why?

With an odd number of voters choosing between north and south, there never would be a tie.

Choose a number less than 10. Now suppose a family with this number of people votes to decide whether to go north or south for a vacation. What are some of the ways that the vote can turn out?

Which of these ways give a clear-cut decision?
Which do not? Why?

Here is a problem for you.

Hold your hands so that your thumbs touch.

How many thumbs are touching? Two.

Now hold your hands so that the next two fingers touch, too. How many fingers are touching?

Try it again with the next two fingers. Then try it again with two more. And the next two. How many fingers are touching? Six and eight and ten.

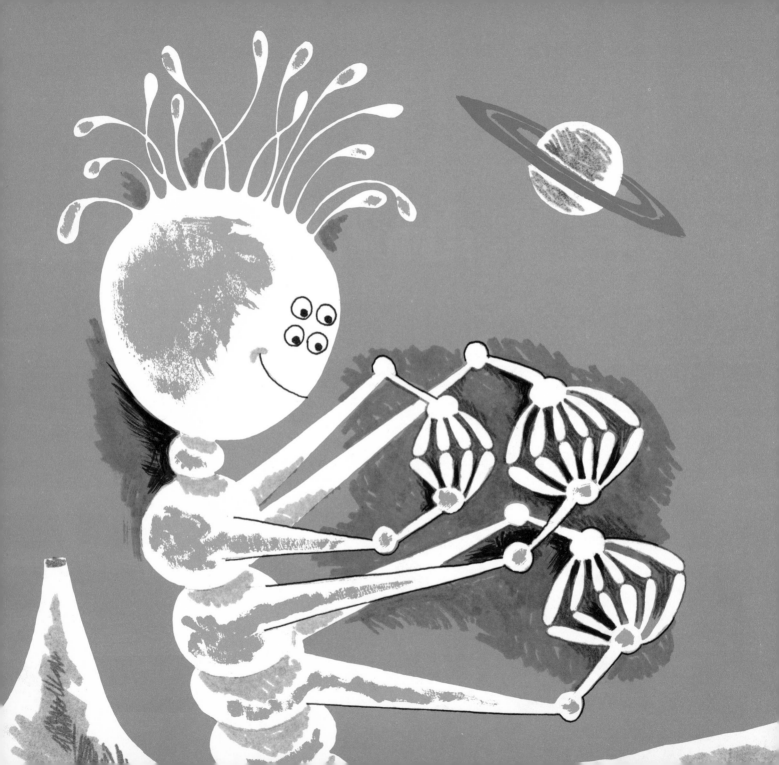

Now suppose you had more fingers on each hand. How many would be touching if you matched them up again? And if you matched once more, how many? If you keep matching fingers this way, what numbers do you get?

What kind of numbers do you get when you match fingers?

Now take 2 blank pieces of paper and put one on top of the other. Take a sharp pencil and push it so that it makes a hole through both pieces of paper. Do it 3 times.

Now count the total number of holes in the 2 sheets of paper. Is it an odd or an even number?

Try making 4 holes through 2 pieces of paper. Count the total number of holes. Is it even or odd? Try 5 holes and do the same thing. Do you get an even or an odd number of holes?

Try more punches. Then count the total number of holes. Do you get an even number or an odd number of holes? What would you have to do to get an odd number?

19

Here is another problem for you. Suppose there is an even number in one group and an even number in another group. How many are there in all? Is it an odd number or an even number? Will your answer always be an even number if each of the groups has an even number?

How about 2 odd-numbered groups? How many are there in all? Is it an even number or an odd number?

Will this always happen, no matter which odd numbers you use? Try it and see.

If one group has 4 members in it and another group has 5 members, is there an even or an odd number in all?

What kind of number do you always get for an answer, if one group has an even number and the other group has an odd number? Why?

We have been talking about odd and even numbers. You have odd and even numbers of things in your body.

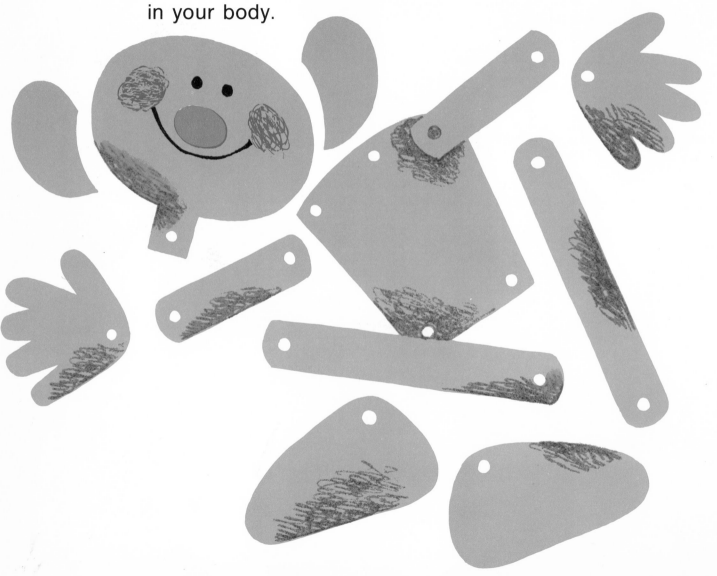

Do you have an odd or an even number of hands?

Do you have an odd or an even number of fingers on one hand? On both hands?

Do you have an odd or an even number of noses? Ears?

What about toes—even or odd?

In your family, is there an even number of hands? Fingers? Noses? Ears? Toes? How can you tell?

Odd and even numbers occur in many places.
Keep an eye open for places where you can find
odd and even numbers of things.

33

ABOUT THE AUTHOR

Thomas C. O'Brien was born in New York City and has received degrees from Iona College, Teachers College, and New York University.

The author of numerous books and articles about both mathematics itself and the teaching of mathematics, Dr. O'Brien is now teaching at Southern Illinois University in Edwardsville, Illinois. He lives not far from the university with his wife, son, and two daughters.

ABOUT THE ILLUSTRATOR

A native of Minnesota, Allan Eitzen attended college and art schools in Minneapolis and Philadelphia. He left art school, shortly after entering, to obtain five years' worth of on-the-job training with a religious publishing company. Mr. Eitzen subsequently finished his schooling and began a successful free-lance career.

Allan Eitzen, his wife, and their five children live in Barto, Pennsylvania, in an old home whose remodeling takes up much of the artist's spare time.